T0115306

The Essential Emily Dickinson

The Essential Emily Dickinson

poems

Selected and with an Introduction
by Joyce Carol Oates

ecco

An imprint of HarperCollinsPublishers

HarperCollins books may be purchased for educational, business, or sales promotional use. For information, please e-mail the Special Markets Department at SPsales@harpercollins.com.

Poems by Emily Dickinson used by special arrangement with the Publishers and the Trustees of Amherst College from THE POEMS OF EMILY DICKINSON, edited by Thomas H. Johnson, Cambridge, Mass.: The Belknap Press of Harvard University Press, Copyright © 1951, 1955 by the President and Fellows of Harvard College. Copyright © renewed 1979, 1983, by the President and Fellows of Harvard College. Copyright © 1914, 1918, 1919, 1924, 1929, 1930, 1932, 1935, 1937, 1942 by Martha Dickinson Bianchi. Copyright © 1952, 1957, 1958, 1963, 1965, by Mary L. Hampson

FIRST ECCO PAPERBACK EDITION PUBLISHED 1996.
SECOND ECCO PAPERBACK EDITION PUBLISHED 2016.

Designed by Nicola Ferguson

Library of Congress Cataloging-in-Publication Data is available upon request.

ISBN 978-0-06-266887-5

23 24 25 26 27 LBC 20 19 18 17 16

CONTENTS

FOREWORD

I HAVE ALWAYS BELIEVED that there is an untapped poetry audience, readers who are just waiting for the kiss of verse to awaken them into a landscape of emotion and image they've never experienced. Contrary to the common cliché, poetry is not actually difficult to understand, on at least one of the many levels a poem may work on—often just the simple, literary level of what the words are saying and what they invoke—"simple truth miscalled simplicity," wrote Shakespeare. Poetry has, and will always, play an important part in our lives. It's obvious to most that during the critical moments in our lives—that would include all rites of passage, from birth, through marriage, to tragedy and death—poetry surfaces to express our deepest feelings, elicits in us a wholeness and depth. A kind of shorthand of the emotions and the soul, a pure form of expression and experience.

So Ecco took it upon itself to go to the keepers of

the flame—they would be the most accomplished poets still living and practicing the art—to pick what is most essential from the canon that has been passed down to us. Thus began Ecco's ESSENTIAL POETS.

It's appropriate that we now celebrate our thirty-fifth anniversary with the reissue of this series, re-packaged but unscathed—a fresh format for the canon's ongoing journey into the hands and hearts of the new readers who will discover the magic in the distillation of this language they inherit. The music of the verbal object.

DANIEL HALPERN
Publisher
Ecco
An Imprint of HarperCollins*Publishers*

INTRODUCTION

BETWEEN THEM, our great visionary poets of the American nineteenth century, Emily Dickinson (1830–1886) and Walt Whitman (1819–1892), have come to represent the extreme, idiosyncratic poles of the American psyche: the intensely inward, private, elliptical and "mystical" (Dickinson); and the robustly outward-looking, public, rhapsodic and "mystical" (Whitman). One declared: "I'm Nobody! Who are you?" The other declared: "Walt Whitman, an American, one of the roughs, a kosmos..." Both were poets whose commitment to poetry was absolute and uncompromising, and whose unconventional lives were so arranged that poetry, "the Soul *at the White Heat*" (Dickinson, 365, ca. 1862), took primacy over all else. (Neither married, for instance, and though Whitman may have boasted of progeny, there are no Whitman children on record. Emily Dickinson was surely celibate through her sequestered life.) When Dickinson died at the age of fifty-five, of Bright's disease, she had lived almost exclusively in her father's house (as she spoke of it) near a busy thoroughfare in the rural town of Amherst, Massachusetts, as a perpetual daughter of the well-to-do household who did not chafe at, but on the contrary celebrated, what she called "the Infinite Power of Home." If it seems almost too symbolically apt that the one great visionary is a woman and the other a man, and that each seems to have wished to promulgate an exaggeration of gender-type (the virgin, the "rough"), it should be emphasized that Dickinson frequently employs a seemingly masculine persona, and most of her poems transcend gender; Whitman is proudly "masculine"—yet his most subtle poems are suffused with an androgynous, even "feminine" sensibility. Dickinson and Whitman can be said to embrace the American cosmos, and their luminous poetry, misunderstood and even repudiated in the poets' lifetimes, possesses a remarkable contemporaneity in our own.

Though it was known among her family and friends that Emily Dickinson had written poems much of her life, the size of the cache discovered by her sister Vinnie after Dickinson's death astonished everyone: 1,775 poems of varying degrees of completeness and legibility, some of them scribbled on the backs of bills. (It was Dickinson's practice to write on scraps of paper that accumulated in her apron pockets during the course of a day, to be artfully assembled at night in the privacy of her room.) So considerable is the poet's posthumous fame that it comes as a revelation to many readers that Dickinson published fewer than twenty poems during her lifetime. Her obscurity as a poet at the time of her death surpassed even that of William Blake, the enigmatic purity of whose *Songs of Innocence and of Experience* suggests a kinship with Dickinson's work. Like the visionary Blake, long considered an eccentric, if not a madman, in the world's eyes, Dickinson was fascinated with the seductive interiority of the imagination: "Within is so wild a place," Dickinson declares. And, in language and imagery Blake would have understood:

> *Much Madness is divinest Sense—*
> *To a discerning Eye—*
> *Much sense—the starkest Madness*
> *'Tis the Majority*
> *In this, as All, prevail—*
>   *(435, ca. 1862)*

Contrary to popular legend, Emily Dickinson was by no means an absolute recluse; she frequently saw a number of Amherst friends and neighbors, participated in a busy household, and maintained friendly relations with several distinguished literary men of the day, two of whom were associated with the Springfield *Daily Republican,* a newspaper of national reputation. The third, T. W. Higginson, a writer for *Atlantic Monthly,* has had the misfortune to enter literary history as the man who failed to recognize Dickinson's genius, but in fact, after Dickinson's death, at the urging of her editor Mabel Loomis Todd, Higginson was instrumental in getting Dickinson's "verse" (as it was condescendingly called) into print. At the time of their primarily epistolary relationship, however, through the 1860s, when Dickinson sent him more than one hundred poems for commentary, Higginson was simply not discerning enough to rise above the conventional poetics of the day: he criticized Dickinson's metrics as "spasmodic" and attempted, with the good intentions of many an obtuse editor confounded by genius, to "correct" her experimental rhyming and syntax. Dickinson dealt with this disappointment by retreating from any active hope of seeing her poetry published, let alone appreciated; her refuge, and her strength, would lie in the subversive strategies of anonymity, invisibility, self-reliance. The poet is indeed, and ideally, "Nobody." Rejection is transposed into defiance: "I'm ceded—I've stopped being Theirs—" (508, ca. 1862). And, in images that conflate poet and female: "They shut me up in Prose—/ As when a Little Girl/ They put me in the Closet—/ Because they liked me 'still'—" (613, ca. 1862).

The poet goes farther, to suggest a radical distinction between two sorts of consciousness, two species of human being:

Best Witchcraft is Geometry
To the magician's mind —
His ordinary acts are feats
To thinking of mankind.

       (1158, ca. 1870)

The witch-poet is the magician of words; ironically, another of her guises is that of a woman of her time, place, and social class. Look for her and she is— where?

I hide myself within my flower
That fading from your Vase,
You, unsuspecting, feel for me —
Almost a loneliness.

       (903, ca. 1864)

In characteristically bold imagery, the poet defines her repressed imagination: "My Life had stood— a Loaded Gun — / In Corners — till a Day / The Owner passed — identified — / And carried Me away —" (754, ca. 1863).

It is believed that Dickinson wrote as many letters as poems, of which approximately 1,000 remain. The letters are as elliptical, rich in imagery, and as teasingly coy as the poems; here is part of a letter of 1862 to her literary friend Samuel Bowles, of the *Daily Republican,* at the time suffering from ill health:

Dear friend.

Are you willing? I am so far from Land—to offer
you the cup—it might some Sabbath come *my*
turn—Of wine how solemn—full!

...While you are sick—we—are homesick—
Do you look out tonight? The Moon rides like a
Girl—through a Topaz Town—I don't think
we shall ever be merry again—you are ill so
long—

When did the Dark happen?

Dickinson discovered, in adolescence, her distinc-
tive voice, and the energies out of which she writes
both poetry and prose are inclined to be roman-
tically adolescent and rebellious; at once self-
effacing and self-declaring. The air of deprivation
that typifies the angrier of the poems is really self-
deprivation, though attributed to other sources.
Hunger—literal? sexual? a hunger for the manly
attributes of freedom and power—is a familiar
motif of the poetry, set forth in brilliantly compact
images:

It would have starved a Gnat
To live so small as I—
And yet I was a living Child—
With Food's necessity

Upon me—like a Claw—
I could no more remove

> *Than I could coax a Leech away —*
> *Or make a Dragon — move*
>
> > *(612, ca. 1862)*

"Gnat" — "Claw" — "Leech" — "Dragon": a child's inventory of monstrous forces to be exorcised; by way of the poet's witchcraft-art, brought into control. For the poet is the "spider" as well, working at night in the secrecy of her room, unwinding a "Yarn of Pearl" unperceived by others and plying "from Nought to Nought/ In unsubstantial Trade —"

> *Dare you see a Soul at the White Heat?*
> *Then crouch within the door —*
> *Red — is the Fire's common tint —*
> *But when the vivid Ore*
> *Has vanquished Flame's conditions,*
> *It quivers from the Forge*
> *Without a color, but the light*
> *Of unanointed Blaze.*
>
> > *(365, ca. 1862)*

Literary fame is perhaps not the goal, but it seems to have been a subject to which the poet has given some thought: "Some — Work for Immortality — / the Chiefer part, for Time —" (406, ca. 1862). And in a flight of speculative discretion:

> *Fame of Myself, to justify,*
> *All other Plaudit be*

Superfluous—An Incense
Beyond Necessity—

Fame of Myself to lack—Although
My Name be else Supreme—
This were an Honor honorless—
A futile Diadem—

(713, ca. 1863)

Yet more wryly in this late, undated poem that might have been written by a poet who had in fact enjoyed public acclaim:

Fame is a bee.
*   It has a song—*
It has a sting—
*   Ah, too, it has a*
wing.

(1763)

And what mysterious eloquence in this similarly late, undated poem, with its powerful Shakespearean resonance:

Fame is a fickle food
Upon a shifting plate
Whose table once a
Guest but not
The second time is set.

Whose crumbs the crows inspect
And with ironic caw
Flap past it to the
Farmer's Corn—
Men eat of it and die.
          (1659)

The poet's willed anonymity/invisibility in her art requires an ascetic paring back of all that is superfluous and distracting and merely "historical" (as opposed to "eternal"). Consequently, much of the external world, the "real" world one might say, is excluded from Dickinson's art; the national disgrace of slavery, the very fact of the Civil War, for instance, are not once named in her poetry though she was writing no less than a poem a day during the terrible years 1862–63. The very antithesis of the public-minded, war-conscious, rhapsodically grieving Walt Whitman! Dickinson never shied away from the great subjects of human suffering, loss, death, even madness, but her perspective was intensely private; like Ranier Maria Rilke and Gerard Manley Hopkins, she is the great poet of inwardness, of that indefinable region of the soul in which we are, in a sense, all one. This is an archetypal world where "Great streets of silence [lead] away/ To Neighborhoods of Pause—" (1159, ca. 1891).

Measured against verse characteristic of her era, Emily Dickinson's poems constitute a kind of counterpoetry. Her miniaturist work is as radical and jarring as Cézanne's landscapes would have seemed to nineteenth-century eyes enamored of the enormous, sublime landscapes of Frederick Edwin Church, Albert Bierstadt, and the Hudson Valley School. Just as the adolescent Emily Dickinson dared to reject Christianity and, in a church-centered village society, declined to attend church services, so too in her art; though she was exceedingly well-read in poetry (Shakespeare, Milton, Byron, Shelley, Goethe, the Brownings, Tennyson, Longfellow, Bryant, Emerson, for instance, as well as lesser, popular poets of her day), she rejected any semblance of orthodoxy. The very look of many of Dickinson's poems on the page is revolutionary: her seemingly breathless pauses and dashes, her odd, Blakean capitalizations, her disjointed phrases and radical variants of rhyme, rhythm, cadence—all point to a poet of unique, unnerving gifts. The signature Dickinson strategy of inverting syntax to call attention to perversities of meaning ("The most obliging Trap/ Its tendency to snap/ Cannot resist" [1340, ca. 1875]) has been traced by scholars to the poet's artful, sometimes playful, adaptation of the rules of Latin grammar for her own purposes. At times, Dickinson seems to anticipate the bold mimicry of childish speech and schizophrenic dreambabble that fascinated James Joyce in the latter part of *Ulysses* and *Finnegans Wake*:

> *This dirty—little—Heart*
> *Is freely mine.*

I won it with a Bun—
A Freckled shrine—

But eligibly fair
To him who sees
The Visage of the Soul
And not the knees.
     (1311, ca. 1874)

Another "modernist" technique in Dickinson is the mimicry of quicksilver moments in which images, thoughts, sensations seem to fly through the poet's mind, recorded in the very instant of their manifestation: "The Red—Blaze—is the Morning—/ The Violet—is Noon—/ The Yellow—Day—is falling—/ And after that—is none—" (469, ca. 1862). And, in its entirety, this koanlike little gem: "The competitions of the sky/ Corrodeless ply." (1494, ca. 1880.) Even in the finely chiseled, much-revised longer poems there is a trompe l'oeil quality, a brilliant mimesis of the ephemera of thought passing through a mind of surpassing discrimination.

Despite the transparency of Dickinson's poetry, in which the "personal" casts but the palest shadow, as in the finely crafted prose of Henry David Thoreau, one has a vivid sense of turbulent emotions, passion, loss. If this is a species of confessional poetry—and what intensely felt poetry is *not* confessional?—it has been purged of all pettiness and self-pity; the poem becomes a vehicle of exorcism through the very precision of its language, as in the much-debated poem whose first stanza is "Wild Nights!—Wild Nights!/ Were I with thee/ Wild Nights should be/ Our luxury!" (249, ca. 1861) but whose conclusion is wholly unexpected. Until fairly recent times in America, as elsewhere, premature death was not uncommon. Nor was it, one supposes, invariably perceived as "premature." Dickinson was literally surrounded by death from childhood onward; the deaths of family members, relatives, friends, and Amherst neighbors; many of them, like her father's, unexpected, and never satisfactorily diagnosed ("apoplexy," the doctor decided). Then there were the slow sinkings-into-death endured by chronic invalids like Dickinson's mother, nursed by her daughter until her death in 1881 when Dickinson was fifty-one years old. Many of Dickinson's most austere, accomplished poems can be considered deathbed or graveside elegies, responses to individual deaths that make no references to the specific; the imagery of death's ceremonial inevitability is never far distant from her imagination: "I felt a Funeral, in my Brain,/And Mourners to and fro" (280, ca. 1861); "Because I could not stop for Death—/ He kindly stopped for me—" (712, ca. 1863); "I heard a Fly buzz—when I died" (341, ca. 1862); "After great pain, a formal feeling comes—" (341, ca. 1862); "What care the Dead, for Chanticleer—/ What care the Dead for Day?" (592, ca. 1862); "I've

seen a Dying Eye/ Run round and round a Room—"
(547, ca. 1862). The poet is both observer and par-
ticipant; death is the greatest of riddles, the most
profound of ironies:

> *To eyelids in the Sepulchre—*
> *How dumb the Dancer lies—*
> *While Color's Revelations break—*
> *And blaze—the butterflies!*
>
> *(496, ca. 1862)*

Dickinson has written as frankly of despair and
the terror of spiritual collapse as any poet who has
ever written, but the poet's cri de coeur transcends
personal anguish to forge convictions, or hypothe-
ses, regarding the general fate of mankind; as in
the extraordinary poems of her most fertile, prolific
decade, the 1860s: "The Brain, within its Groove"
(556, ca. 1862); "There is a pain—so utter—/ It
swallows substance up—" (599, ca. 1862); "I felt a
Cleaving in my Mind—/ As if my Brain had split—"
(937, ca. 1864); and, most terrifying of all, in the
very grace of its utterance, "The first Day's Night
had come—" (410, ca. 1862). And what tranquility
of resignation, beyond tragedy, in this poem of two
packed lines:

> *To Whom the Mornings stand for Nights,*
> *What must the Midnights—be!*
>
> *(1095, ca. 1866)*

And this heartrending aside, in the midst of an elegy:

> Oh Life, begun in fluent Blood,
> And consummated dull!
> *(1130, ca. 1868)*

Yet there is a side of Emily Dickinson that is not elegiac, nor even stoic and "profound"; her temperament was as much subversively playful as solemn, and even rather wicked, as in a number of her frankly funny asides on persons, customs, reigning orthodoxies she has observed. The first poem in this anthology, written when Dickinson was nineteen years old, suggests both her precocious skill as a young poet and her mordant sense of humor ("The *worm* doth woo the *mortal,* death claims a living bride"); it demonstrates how confidently she could craft "verse" in swinging couplets. And how wise she was, to abandon the genre forever. I include it here, along with other of Dickinson's genial parodies and comic takes ("A Charm invests a face/ Imperfectly beheld—" [421, ca. 1862]) and corrosive theological aphorisms ("...The Maker's cordial visage,/ However good to see,/ Is shunned, we must admit it,/ Like an adversity" [1718, ca. ?]) to give the reader a sense of Dickinson's generally unacknowledged variation of voice; and, of course, because the poems merit attention. It seems instructive to know that in the year of miracles in which so many of her great elegiac poems were composed, 1862, Dickinson was capable of a sly good humor:

> What Soft—Cherubic Creatures—
> These Gentlewomen are—
> One would as soon assault a Plush—
> Or violate a Star—
>
> (401, ca. 1862)

(How intriguing to note that, in these lines, the poet distinguishes herself from "gentlewomen" as from another species; and fantasizes, as from a male perspective, their "violation"!)

At the last, on her very deathbed, it was the droll miniaturist Dickinson who contemplated her fate, composing a final letter that reads as a perfect little poem, a gesture of the gentlest irony:

> Little Cousins—
> Called back—
> Emily.
> (May 1885)

Called Back was the title of a popular sentimental religious novel of the time, but it was, more significantly, a printer's term: printed material would be "called back" if typographical errors had been discovered.

THERE IS no poet, and particularly no American poet, who has not been touched by Emily Dickinson. Like the flamboyant Dylan Thomas, though she is a far greater poet than Thomas, Dickinson is immensely seductive to young poets; one can admire her passionately, one can have virtually memorized any number of her poems, yet to be "influenced" by her is simply not possible. She is sui generis. To be influenced by Dickinson, as by Dylan Thomas, is a fatal error. (Unless, of course, one is a poet of genius oneself, like William Carlos Williams. Or, in her own mordant way, Sylvia Plath.)

I began reading Emily Dickinson as an adolescent, and have continued through my life; her work retains, for me, the drama and "white-hot" intensity of adolescence, like the work of Henry David Thoreau. Certain of Dickinson's poems are very likely more deeply imprinted in my soul than they were ever imprinted in the poet's, and inevitably they reside more deeply, and more mysteriously, than much of my own work. For the writer is, as Dickinson's poetpersona suggests, a creature forever in motion, calculating and breathless at once; casting out demons, joy, gems, "profundity" in skeins of language, then moving restlessly on. Her work, if it endures at all, can only endure, in Auden's striking phrase, "in the guts of the living."

The *Essential Dickinson* is, I suppose, a personal

selection—yet not a private one. It includes the poems generally considered great—and they are many. It contains the much-anthologized; but it also contains the virtually never anthologized. Dickinson is one of very few poets whose work repays countless readings, through a lifetime. I am continually discovering poems I'd believed I knew, seeing them in a different light, from a different perspective. We return to Dickinson for that magical experience so famously described by Dickinson herself, in a letter to her would-be mentor T. W. Higginson:

> If I read a book [and] it makes my whole body so cold no fire can ever warm me I know that is poetry. If I feel physically as if the top of my head were taken off, I know *that* is poetry. These are the only way [sic] I know it. Is there any other way.

—*JOYCE CAROL OATES*

The Essential Emily Dickinson

POEMS

1

Valentine week

Awake ye muses nine, sing me a strain divine,
Unwind the solemn twine, and tie my Valentine!

Oh the Earth was *made* for lovers, for damsel, and
    hopeless swain,
For sighing, and gentle whispering, and *unity* made
    of *twain*.
All things do go a courting, in earth, or sea, or air,
God hath made nothing single but *thee* in His world
    so fair!
The *bride*, and then the *bridegroom*, the *two*, and then
    the *one*,
Adam, and Eve, his consort, the moon, and then
    the sun;

The life doth prove the precept, who obey shall
    happy be,
Who will not serve the sovereign, be hanged on fatal
    tree.
The high do seek the lowly, the great do seek the
    small,
None cannot find who *seeketh*, on this terrestial ball;
The bee doth court the flower, the flower his suit
    receives,
And they make merry wedding, whose guests are
    hundred leaves;
The wind doth woo the branches, the branches they
    are won,
And the father fond demandeth the maiden for
    his son.
The storm doth walk the seashore humming a
    mournful tune,
The wave with eye so pensive, looketh to see the
    moon,
Their spirits meet together, they make them solemn
    vows,
No more he singeth mournful, her sadness she doth
    lose.
The *worm* doth woo the *mortal*, death claims a living
    bride,
Night unto day is married, morn unto eventide;
Earth is a merry damsel, and *heaven* a knight so true,
And Earth is quite coquettish, and beseemeth in
    vain to sue.
Now to the *application*, to the reading of the roll,

To bringing thee to justice, and marshalling thy
   soul:
Thou art a *human* solo, a being cold, and lone,
Wilt have no kind companion, thou *reap'st* what
   thou has *sown*.
Hast never silent hours, and minutes all too long,
And a deal of sad reflection, and *wailing* instead of
   song?
There's *Sarah,* and *Eliza,* and *Emeline* so fair,
And *Harriet,* and *Susan,* and she with *curling hair!*
Thine eyes are sadly blinded, but yet thou mayest
   see
Six true, and comely maidens sitting upon the tree;
Approach that tree with caution, then up it boldly
   climb,
And seize the one thou lovest, nor care for *space,* or
   time!
Then bear her to the greenwood, and build for her
   a bower,
And give her what she asketh, jewel, or bird, or
   flower —
And bring the fife, and trumpet, and beat upon the
   drum —
And bid the world Goodmorrow, and go to glory
   home!

67

Success is counted sweetest
By those who ne'er succeed.
To comprehend a nectar
Requires sorest need.

Not one of all the purple Host
Who took the Flag today
Can tell the definition
So clear of Victory

As he defeated—dying—
On whose forbidden ear
The distant strains of triumph
Burst agonized and clear!

130

These are the days when Birds come back—
A very few—a Bird or two—
To take a backward look.

These are the days when skies resume
The old—old sophistries of June—
A blue and gold mistake.

Oh fraud that cannot cheat the Bee—
Almost thy plausibility
Induces my belief.

Till ranks of seeds their witness bear—
And softly thro' the altered air
Hurries a timid leaf.

Oh Sacrament of summer days,
Oh Last Communion in the Haze—
Permit a child to join.

Thy sacred emblems to partake—
Thy consecrated bread to take
And thine immortal wine!

135

Water, is taught by thirst.
Land—by the Oceans passed.
Transport—by throe—
Peace—by it's battles told—
Love, by Memorial Mold—
Birds, by the Snow.

156

You love me—you are sure—
I shall not fear mistake—
I shall not *cheated* wake—
Some grinning morn—

To find the Sunrise left—
And Orchards—unbereft—
And Dollie—gone!

I need not start—you're sure—
That night will never be—
When frightened—home to Thee I run—
To find the windows dark—
And no more Dollie—mark—
Quite none?

Be sure you're sure—you know—
I'll bear it better now—
If you'll just tell me so—
Than when—a little dull Balm grown—
Over this pain of mine—
You sting—again!

165

A *Wounded* Deer—leaps highest—
I've heard the Hunter tell—
'Tis but the Extasy of *death*—
And then the Brake is still!

The *Smitten* Rock that gushes!
The *trampled* Steel that springs!
A Cheek is always redder
Just where the Hectic stings!

Mirth is the Mail of Anguish —
In which it Cautious Arm,
Lest anybody spy the blood
And "you're hurt" exclaim!

185

"Faith" is a fine invention
When Gentlemen can *see* —
But *Microscopes* are prudent
In an Emergency.

199

I'm "wife" — I've finished that —
That other state —
I'm Czar — I'm "Woman" now —
It's safer so —

How odd the Girl's life looks
Behind this soft Eclipse —
I think that Earth feels so
To folks in Heaven — now —

This being comfort — then
That other kind — was pain —
But why compare?
I'm "Wife"! Stop there!

214

I taste a liquor never brewed—
From Tankards scooped in Pearl—
Not all the Frankfort Berries
Yield such an Alcohol!

Inebriate of Air—am I—
And Debauchee of Dew—
Reeling—thro endless summer days—
From inns of Molten Blue—

When "Landlords" turn the drunken Bee
Out of the Foxglove's door—
When Butterflies—renounce their "drams"—
I shall but drink the more!

Till Seraphs swing their snowy Hats—
And Saints—to windows run—
To see the little Tippler
From Manzanilla come!

216

Safe in their Alabaster Chambers—
Untouched by Morning
And untouched by Noon—
Sleep the meek members of the Resurrection—
Rafter of satin,
And Roof of stone.

Light laughs the breeze
In her Castle above them—
Babbles the Bee in a stolid Ear,
Pipe the Sweet Birds in ignorant cadence—
Ah, what sagacity perished here!

version of 1859

Safe in their Alabaster Chambers—
Untouched by Morning—
And untouched by Noon—
Lie the meek members of the Resurrection—
Rafter of Satin—and Roof of Stone!

Grand go the Years—in the Crescent—
    above them—
Worlds scoop their Arcs—
And Firmaments—row—
Diadems—drop—and Doges—surrender—
Soundless as dots—on a Disc of Snow—

version of 1861

241

I like a look of Agony,
Because I know it's true—
Men do not sham Convulsion,
Nor simulate, a Throe—

The Eyes glaze once—and that is Death—
Impossible to feign

The Beads upon the Forehead
By homely Anguish strung.

249

Wild Nights — Wild Nights!
Were I with thee
Wild Nights should be
Our luxury!

Futile — the Winds —
To a Heart in port —
Done with the Compass —
Done with the Chart!

Rowing in Eden —
Ah, the Sea!
Might I but moor — Tonight —
In Thee!

252

I can wade Grief —
Whole Pools of it —
I'm used to that —
But the least push of Joy
Breaks up my feet —
And I tip — drunken —

Let no Pebble — smile —
'Twas the New Liquor —
That was all!

Power is only Pain —
Stranded, thro'Discipline,
Till Weights — will hang —
Give Balm — to Giants —
And they'll wilt, like Men —
Give Himmaleh —
They'll Carry — Him!

254

"Hope" is the thing with feathers —
That perches in the soul —
And sings the tune without the words —
And never stops — at all —

And sweetest — in the Gale — is heard —
And sore must be the storm —
That could abash the little Bird
That kept so many warm —

I've heard it in the chillest land —
And on the strangest Sea —
Yet, never, in Extremity,
It asked a crumb — of Me.

There's a certain Slant of light,
Winter Afternoons —
That oppresses, like the Heft
Of Cathedral Tunes —

Heavenly Hurt, it gives us —
We can find no scar,
But internal difference,
Where the Meanings, are —

None may teach it — Any —
'Tis the Seal Despair —
An imperial affliction
Sent us of the Air —

When it comes, the Landscape listens —
Shadows — hold their breath —
When it goes, 'tis like the Distance
On the look of Death —

280

I felt a Funeral, in my Brain,
And Mourners to and fro
Kept treading — treading — till it seemed
That Sense was breaking through —

And when they all were seated,
A Service, like a Drum—
Kept beating—beating—till I thought
My Mind was going numb—

And then I heard them lift a Box
And creak across my Soul
With those same Boots of Lead, again,
Then Space—began to toll,

As all the Heavens were a Bell,
And Being, but an Ear,
And I, and Silence, some strange Race
Wrecked, solitary, here—

And then a Plank in Reason, broke,
And I dropped down, and down—
And hit a World, at every plunge,
And Finished knowing—then—

288

I'm Nobody! Who are you?
Are you—Nobody—too?
Then there's a pair of us!
Don't tell! they'd banish us—you know!

How dreary—to be—Somebody!
How public—like a Frog—

To tell your name—the livelong June—
To an admiring Bog!

294

The Doomed—regard the Sunrise
With different Delight—
Because—when next it burns abroad
They doubt to witness it—

The Man—to die—tomorrow—
Harks for the Meadow Bird—
Because it's Music stirs the Axe
That clamors for his head—

Joyful—to whom the Sunrise
Precedes Enamored—Day—
Joyful—for whom the Meadow Bird
Has ought but Elegy!

303

The Soul selects her own Society—
Then—shuts the Door—
To her divine Majority—
Present no more—

Unmoved—she notes the Chariots—pausing—
At her low Gate—
Unmoved—an Emperor be kneeling
Upon her Mat—

I've known her—from an ample nation—
Choose One—
Then—close the Valves of her attention—
Like Stone—

305

The difference between Despair
And Fear—is like the One
Between the instant of a Wreck—
And when the Wreck has been—

The Mind is smooth—no Motion—
Contented as the Eye
Upon the Forehead of a Bust—
That knows—it cannot see—

315

He fumbles at your Soul
As Players at the Keys
Before they drop full Music on—

He stuns you by degrees —
Prepares your brittle Nature
For the Ethereal Blow
By fainter Hammers — further heard —
Then nearer — Then so slow
Your Breath has time to straighten —
Your Brain — to bubble Cool —
Deals — One — imperial — Thunderbolt —
That scalps your naked Soul —

When Winds take Forests in their Paws —
The Universe — is still —

320

We play at Paste —
Till qualified, for Pearl —
Then, drop the Paste —
And deem ourself a fool —

The Shapes — though — were similar —
And our new Hands
Learned *Gem*-Tactics —
Practicing *Sands*—

Before I got my eye put out
I liked as well to see—
As other Creatures, that have Eyes
And know no other way—

But were it told to me—Today—
That I might have the sky
For mine—I tell you that my Heart
Would split, for size of me—

The Meadows—mine—
The Mountains—mine—
All Forests—Stintless Stars—
As much of Noon as I could take
Between my finite eyes—

The Motions of The Dipping Birds—
The Morning's Amber Road—
For mine—to look at when I liked—
The News would strike me dead—

So safer Guess—with just my soul
Upon the Window pane—
Where other Creatures put their eyes—
Incautious—of the Sun—

A Bird came down the Walk—
He did not know I saw—
He bit an Angleworm in halves
And ate the fellow, raw,

And then he drank a Dew
From a convenient Grass—
And then hopped sidewise to the Wall
To let a Beetle pass—

He glanced with rapid eyes
That hurried all around—
They looked like frightened Beads, I thought—
He stirred his Velvet Head

Like one in danger, Cautious,
I offered him a Crumb
And he unrolled his feathers
And rowed him softer home—

Than Oars divide the Ocean,
Too silver for a seam—
Or Butterflies, off Banks of Noon
Leap, plashless as they swim.

341

After great pain, a formal feeling comes—
The Nerves sit ceremonious, like Tombs—
The stiff Heart questions was it He, that bore,
And Yesterday, or Centuries before?

The Feet, mechanical, go round—
Of Ground, or Air, or Ought—
A Wooden way
Regardless grown,
A Quartz contentment, like a stone—

This is the Hour of Lead—
Remembered, if outlived,
As Freezing persons, recollect the Snow—
First—Chill—then Stupor—then the letting go—

360

Death sets a Thing significant
The Eye had hurried by
Except a perished Creature
Entreat us tenderly

To ponder little Workmanships
In Crayon, or in Wool,
With "This was last Her fingers did"—
Industrious until—

The Thimble weighed too heavy—
The stitches stopped—themselves—
And then 'twas put among the Dust
Upon the Closet shelves—

A Book I have—a friend gave—
Whose Pencil—here and there—
Had notched the place that pleased Him—
At Rest—His fingers are—

Now—when I read—I read not—
For interrupting Tears—
Obliterate the Etchings
Too Costly for Repairs.

364

The Morning after Wo—
'Tis frequently the Way—
Surpasses all that rose before—
For utter Jubilee—

As Nature did not care—
And piled her Blossoms on—
And further to parade a Joy
Her Victim stared upon—

The Birds declaim their Tunes—
Pronouncing every word

Like Hammers — Did they know they fell
Like Litanies of Lead —

On here and there — a creature —
They'd modify the Glee
To fit some Crucifixal Clef —
Some Key of Calvary —

365

Dare you see a Soul *at the White Heat*?
Then crouch within the door —
Red — is the Fire's common tint —
But when the vivid Ore
Has vanquished Flame's conditions,
It quivers from the Forge
Without a color, but the light
Of unannointed Blaze.
Least Village has it's Blacksmith
Whose Anvil's even ring
Stands symbol for the finer Forge
That soundless tugs — within —
Refining these impatient Ores
With Hammer, and with Blaze
Until the Designated Light
Repudiate the Forge —

There's been a Death, in the Opposite House,
As lately as Today—
I know it, by the numb look
Such Houses have—alway—

The Neighbors rustle in and out—
The Doctor—drives away—
A Window opens like a Pod—
Abrupt—mechanically—

Somebody flings a Mattrass out—
The Children hurry by—
They wonder if it died—on that—
I used to—when a Boy—

The Minister—goes stiffly in—
As if the House were His—
And He owned all the Mourners—now—
And little Boys—besides—

And then the Milliner—and the Man
Of the Appalling Trade—
To take the measure of the House—

There'll be that Dark Parade—

Of Tassels—and of Coaches—soon—
It's easy as a Sign—

The Intuition of the News—
In just a Country Town—

396

There is a Languor of the Life
More imminent than Pain—
'Tis Pain's Successor—When the Soul
Has suffered all it can—

A Drowsiness—diffuses—
A Dimness like a Fog
Envelopes Consciousness—
As Mists—obliterate a Crag.

The Surgeon—does not blanch—at pain—
His Habit—is severe—
But tell him that it ceased to feel—
The Creature lying there—

And he will tell you—skill is late—
A Mightier than He—
Has ministered before Him—
There's no Vitality

401

What Soft—Cherubic Creatures—
These Gentlewomen are—
One would as soon assault a Plush—
Or violate a Star—

Such Dimity Convictions—
A Horror so refined
Of freckled Human Nature—
Of Deity—ashamed—

It's such a common—Glory—
A Fisherman's—Degree—
Redemption—Brittle Lady—
Be so—ashamed of Thee—

410

The first Day's Night had come—
And grateful that a thing
So terrible—had been endured—
I told my Soul to sing—

She said her Strings were snapt—
Her Bow—to Atoms blown—
And so to mend her—gave me work
Until another Morn—

And then — a Day as huge
As Yesterdays in pairs,
Unrolled it's horror in my face —
Until it blocked my eyes —

My Brain — begun to laugh —
I mumbled — like a fool —
And tho' 'tis Years ago — that Day —
My Brain keeps giggling — still.

And Something's odd — within —
That person that I was —
And this One — do not feel the same —
Could it be Madness — this?

414

'Twas like a Maelstrom, with a notch,
That nearer, every Day,
Kept narrowing it's boiling Wheel
Until the Agony

Toyed coolly with the final inch
Of your delirious Hem —
And you dropt, lost,
When something broke —
And let you from a Dream —

As if a Goblin with a Guage —
Kept measuring the Hours —
Until you felt your Second
Weigh, helpless, in his Paws —

And not a Sinew — stirred — could help,
And sense was setting numb —
When God — remembered — and the Fiend
Let go, then, Overcome —

As if your Sentence stood — pronounced —
And you were frozen led
From Dungeon's luxury of Doubt
To Gibbets, and the Dead —

And when the Film had stitched your eyes
A Creature gasped "Repreive"!
Which Anguish was the utterest — then —
To perish, or to live?

419

We grow accustomed to the Dark —
When Light is put away —
As when the Neighbor holds the Lamp
To witness her Goodbye —

A Moment — We uncertain step
For newness of the night —

Then—fit our Vision to the Dark—
And meet the Road—erect—

And so of larger—Darknesses—
Those Evenings of the Brain—
When not a Moon disclose a sign—
Or Star—come out—within—

The B[r]avest—grope a little—
And sometimes hit a Tree
Directly in the Forehead—
But as they learn to see—

Either the Darkness alters—
Or something in the sight
Adjusts itself to Midnight—
And Life steps almost straight.

421

A Charm invests a face
Imperfectly beheld—
The Lady dare not lift her Vail
For fear it be dispelled—

But peers beyond her mesh—
And wishes—and denies—
Lest Interview—annul a want
That Image—satisfies—

425

Good Morning—Midnight—
I'm coming Home—
Day—got tired of Me—
How could I—of Him?

Sunshine was a sweet place—
I liked to stay—
But Morn—did'nt want me—now—
So—Goodnight—Day!

I can look—cant I—
When the East is Red?
The Hills—have a way—then—
That puts the Heart—abroad—

You—are not so fair—Midnight—
I chose—Day—
But—please take a little Girl—
He turned away!

435

Much Madness is divinest Sense—
To a discerning Eye—
Much Sense—the starkest Madness—
'Tis the Majority
In this, as All, prevail—

Assent—and you are sane—
Demur—you're straightway dangerous—
And handled with a Chain—

441

This is my letter to the World
That never wrote to Me—
The simple News that Nature told—
With tender Majesty

Her Message is committed
To Hands I cannot see—
For love of Her—Sweet—countrymen—
Judge tenderly—of Me

449

I died for Beauty—but was scarce
Adjusted in the Tomb
When One who died for Truth, was lain
In an adjoining Room—

He questioned softly "Why I failed"?
"For Beauty", I replied—
"And I—for Truth—Themself are One—
We Bretheren, are", He said—

And so, as Kinsmen, met a Night—
We talked between the Rooms—
Until the Moss had reached our lips—
And covered up—our names—

451

The Outer—from the Inner
Derives it's Magnitude—
'Tis Duke, or Dwarf, according
As is the Central Mood—

The fine—unvarying Axis
That regulates the Wheel—
Though Spokes—spin—more conspicuous
And fling a dust—the while.

The Inner—paints the Outer—
The Brush without the Hand—
It's Picture publishes—precise—
As is the inner Brand—

On fine—Arterial Canvas—
A Cheek—perchance a Brow—
The Star's whole Secret—in the Lake—
Eyes were not meant to know.

A Wife — at Daybreak I shall be —
Sunrise — Hast thou a Flag for me?
At Midnight, I am but a Maid,
How short it takes to make it Bride —
Then — Midnight, I have passed from thee
Unto the East, and Victory —

Midnight — Good Night! I hear them call,
The Angels bustle in the Hall —
Softly my Future climbs the Stair,
I fumble at my Childhood's prayer
So soon to be a Child no more —
Eternity, I'm coming — Sir,
Savior — I've seen the face — before!

465

I heard a Fly buzz — when I died —
The Stillness in the Room
Was like the Stillness in the Air —
Between the Heaves of Storm —

The Eyes around — had wrung them dry —
And Breaths were gathering firm
For that last Onset — when the King
Be witnessed — in the Room —

I willed my Keepsakes — Signed away
What portion of me be
Assignable — and then it was
There interposed a Fly —

With Blue — uncertain stumbling Buzz —
Between the light — and me —
And then the Windows failed — and then
I could not see to see —

469

The Red — Blaze — is the Morning —
The Violet — is Noon —
The Yellow — Day — is falling —
And after that — is none —

But Miles of Sparks — at Evening —
Reveal the Width that burned —
The Territory Argent — that
Never yet — consumed —

479

She dealt her pretty words like Blades —
How glittering they shone —
And every One unbared a Nerve
Or wantoned with a Bone —

She never deemed—she hurt—
That—is not Steel's Affair—
A vulgar grimace in the Flesh—
How ill the Creatures bear—

To Ache is human—not polite—
The Film upon the eye
Mortality's old Custom—
Just locking up—to Die.

501

This World is not Conclusion.
A Species stands beyond—
Invisible, as Music—
But positive, as Sound—
It beckons, and it baffles—
Philosophy—dont know—
And through a Riddle, at the last—
Sagacity, must go—
To guess it, puzzles scholars—
To gain it, Men have borne
Contempt of Generations
And Crucifixion, shown—
Faith slips—and laughs, and rallies—
Blushes, if any see—
Plucks at a twig of Evidence—
And asks a Vane, the way—
Much Gesture, from the Pulpit—

Strong Hallelujahs roll—
Narcotics cannot still the Tooth
That nibbles at the soul—

507

She sights a Bird—she chuckles—
She flattens—then she crawls—
She runs without the look of feet—
Her eyes increase to Balls—

Her Jaws stir—twitching—hungry—
Her Teeth can hardly stand—
She leaps, but Robin leaped the first—
Ah, Pussy, of the Sand,

The Hopes so juicy ripening—
You almost bathed your Tongue—
When Bliss disclosed a hundred Toes—
And fled with every one—

508

I'm ceded—I've stopped being Their's—
The name They dropped upon my face
With water, in the country church
Is finished using, now,

And They can put it with my Dolls,
My childhood, and the string of spools,
I've finished threading — too —

Baptized, before, without the choice,
But this time, consciously, of Grace —
Unto supremest name —
Called to my Full — The Crescent dropped —
Existence's whole Arc, filled up,
With one small Diadem.

My second Rank — too small the first —
Crowned — Crowing — on my Father's breast —
A half unconscious Queen —
But this time — Adequate — Erect,
With Will to choose, or to reject,
And I choose, just a Crown —

510

It was not Death, for I stood up,
And all the Dead, lie down —
It was not Night, for all the Bells
Put out their Tongues, for Noon.

It was not Frost, for on my Flesh
I felt Siroccos — crawl —
Nor Fire — for just my Marble feet
Could keep a Chancel, cool —

And yet, it tasted, like them all,
The Figures I have seen
Set orderly, for Burial,
Reminded me, of mine—

As if my life were shaven,
And fitted to a frame,
And could not breathe without a key,
And 'twas like Midnight, some—

When everything that ticked—has stopped—
And Space stares all around—
Or Grisly frosts—first Autumn morns,
Repeal the Beating Ground—

But, most, like Chaos—Stopless—cool—
Without a Chance, or Spar—
Or even a Report of Land—
To justify—Despair.

512

The Soul has Bandaged moments—
When too appalled to stir—
She feels some ghastly Fright come up
And stop to look at her—

Salute her—with long fingers—
Caress her freezing hair—

Sip, Goblin, from the very lips
The Lover—hovered—o'er—
Unworthy, that a thought so mean
Accost a Theme—so—fair—

The soul has moments of Escape—
When bursting all the doors—
She dances like a Bomb, abroad,
And swings upon the Hours,

As do the Bee—delirious borne—
Long Dungeoned from his Rose—
Touch Liberty—then know no more,
But Noon, and Paradise—

The Soul's retaken moments—
When, Felon led along,
With shackles on the plumed feet,
And staples, in the Song,

The Horror welcomes her, again,
These, are not brayed of Tongue—

520

I started Early—Took my Dog—
And visited the Sea—
The Mermaids in the Basement
Came out to look at me—

And Frigates—in the Upper Floor
Extended Hempen Hands—
Presuming Me to be a Mouse—
Aground—upon the Sands—

But no Man moved Me—till the Tide
Went past my simple Shoe—
And past my Apron—and my Belt
And past my Bodice—too—

And made as He would eat me up—
As wholly as a Dew
Upon a Dandelion's Sleeve—
And then—I started—too—

And He—He followed—close behind—
I felt His Silver Heel
Upon my Ankle—Then my Shoes
Would overflow with Pearl—

Until We met the Solid Town—
No One He seemed to know—
And bowing—with a Mighty look—
At me—The Sea withdrew—

532

I tried to think a lonelier Thing
Than any I had seen—

Some Polar Expiation—An Omen in the Bone
Of Death's tremendous nearness—

I probed Retrieveless things
My Duplicate—to borrow—
A Haggard Comfort springs

From the belief that Somewhere—
Within the Clutch of Thought—
There dwells one other Creature
Of Heavenly Love—forgot—

I plucked at our Partition
As One should pry the Walls—
Between Himself—and Horror's Twin—
Within Opposing Cells—

I almost strove to clasp his Hand,
Such Luxury—it grew—
That as Myself—could pity Him—
Perhaps he—pitied me—

547

I've seen a Dying Eye
Run round and round a Room—
In search of Something—as it seemed—
Then Cloudier become—
And then—obscure with Fog—

And then—be soldered down
Without disclosing what it be
'Twere blessed to have seen—

556

The Brain, within it's Groove
Runs evenly—and true—
But let a Splinter swerve—
'Twere easier for You—

To put a Current back—
When Floods have slit the Hills—
And scooped a Turnpike for Themselves—
And trodden out the Mills—

561

I measure every Grief I meet
With narrow, probing, Eyes—
I wonder if It weighs like Mine—
Or has an Easier size.

I wonder if They bore it long—
Or did it just begin—
I could not tell the Date of Mine—
It feels so old a pain—

I wonder if it hurts to live—
And if They have to try—
And whether—could They choose between—
It would not be—to die—

I note that Some—gone patient long—
At length, renew their smile—
An imitation of a Light
That has so little Oil—

I wonder if when Years have piled—
Some Thousands—on the Harm—
That hurt them early—such a lapse
Could give them any Balm—

Or would they go on aching still
Through Centuries of Nerve—
Enlightened to a larger Pain—
In Contrast with the Love—

The Grieved—are many—I am told—
There is the various Cause—
Death—is but one—and comes but once—
And only nails the eyes—

There's Grief of Want—and Grief of Cold—
A sort they call "Despair"—
There's Banishment from native Eyes—
In sight of Native Air—

And though I may not guess the kind—
Correctly—yet to me
A piercing Comfort it affords
In passing Calvary—

To note the fashions—of the Cross—
And how they're mostly worn—
Still fascinated to presume
That Some—are like My Own—

579

I had been hungry, all the Years—
My Noon had Come—to dine—
I trembling drew the Table near—
And touched the Curious Wine—

'Twas this on Tables I had seen—
When turning, hungry, Home
I looked in Windows, for the Wealth
I could not hope—for Mine—

I did not know the ample Bread—
'Twas so unlike the Crumb
The Birds and I, had often shared
In Nature's—Dining Room—

The Plenty hurt me—'twas so new—
Myself felt ill—and odd—

As Berry—of a Mountain Bush—
Transplanted—to the Road—

Nor was I hungry—so I found
That Hunger—was a way
Of Persons outside Windows—
The Entering—takes away—

593

I think I was enchanted
When first a sombre Girl—
I read that Foreign Lady—
The Dark—felt beautiful—

And whether it was noon at night—
Or only Heaven—at Noon—
For very Lunacy of Light
I had not power to tell—

The Bees—became as Butterflies—
The Butterflies—as Swans—
Approached—and spurned the narrow Grass—
And just the meanest Tunes.

That Nature murmured to herself
To keep herself in Cheer—
I took for Giants—practising
Titanic Opera—

The Days—to Mighty Metres stept—
The Homeliest—adorned
As if unto a Jubilee
'Twere suddenly confirmed—

I could not have defined the change—
Conversion of the Mind
Like Sanctifying in the Soul—
Is witnessed—not explained—

'Twas a Divine Insanity—
The Danger to be Sane
Should I again experience—
'Tis Antidote to turn—

To Tomes of solid Witchcraft—
Magicians be asleep—
But Magic—hath an Element
Like Deity—to keep—

599

There is a pain—so utter—
It swallows substance up—
Then covers the Abyss with Trance—
So Memory can step

Around—across—upon it—
As one within a Swoon—

Goes safely—where an open eye—
Would drop Him—Bone by Bone.

605

The Spider holds a Silver Ball
In unperceived Hands—
And dancing softly to Himself
His Yarn of Pearl—unwinds—

He plies from Nought to Nought—
In unsubstantial Trade—
Supplants our Tapestries with His—
In half the period—

An Hour to rear supreme
His Continents of Light—
Then dangle from the Housewife's Broom—
His Boundaries—forgot—

607

Of nearness to her sundered Things
The Soul has special times—
When Dimness—looks the Oddity—
Distinctness—easy—seems—

The Shapes we buried, dwell about,
Familiar, in the Rooms—

Untarnished by the Sepulchre,
The Mouldering Playmate comes —

In just the Jacket that he wore —
Long buttoned in the Mold
Since we — old mornings, Children — played —
Divided — by a world —

The Grave yields back her Robberies —
The Years, our pilfered Things —
Bright Knots of Apparitions
Salute us, with their wings —

As we — it were — that perished —
Themself — had just remained till we rejoin them —
And 'twas they, and not ourself
That mourned.

609

I Years had been from Home
And now before the Door
I dared not enter, lest a Face
I never saw before

Stare stolid into mine
And ask my Business there —
"My Business but a Life I left
Was such remaining there?"

I leaned upon the Awe—
I lingered with Before—
The Second like an Ocean rolled
And broke against my ear—

I laughed a crumbling Laugh
That I could fear a Door
Who Consternation compassed
And never winced before.

I fitted to the Latch
My Hand, with trembling care
Lest back the awful Door should spring
And leave me in the Floor—

Then moved my Fingers off
As cautiously as Glass
And held my ears, and like a Thief
Fled gasping from the House—

613

They shut me up in Prose—
As when a Little Girl
They put me in the Closet—
Because they liked me "still"—

Still! Could themself have peeped—
And seen my Brain—go round—

They might as wise have lodged a Bird
For Treason — in the Pound —

Himself has but to will
And easy as a Star
Look down upon Captivity —
And laugh — No more have I —

627

The Tint I cannot take — is best —
The Color too remote
That I could show it in Bazaar —
A Guinea at a sight —

The fine — impalpable Array —
That swaggers on the eye
Like Cleopatra's Company —
Repeated — in the sky —

The Moments of Dominion
That happen on the Soul
And leave it with a Discontent
Too exquisite — to tell —

The eager look — on Landscapes —
As if they just repressed
Some Secret — that was pushing
Like Chariots — in the Vest —

The Pleading of the Summer—
That other Prank—of Snow—
That Cushions Mystery with Tulle,
For fear the Squirrels—know.

Their Graspless manners—mock us—
Until the Cheated Eye
Shuts arrogantly—in the Grave—
Another way—to see—

632

The Brain—is wider than the Sky—
For—put them side by side—
The one the other will contain
With ease—and You—beside—

The Brain is deeper than the sea—
For—hold them—Blue to Blue—
The one the other will absorb—
As Sponges—Buckets—do—

The Brain is just the weight of God—
For—Heft them—Pound for Pound—
And they will differ—if they do—
As Syllable from Sound—

I cannot live with You—
It would be Life—
And Life is over there—
Behind the Shelf

The Sexton keeps the Key to—
Putting up
Our Life—His Porcelain—
Like a Cup—

Discarded of the Housewife—
Quaint—or Broke—
A newer Sevres pleases—
Old Ones crack—

I could not die—with You—
For One must wait
To shut the Other's Gaze down—
You—could not—

And I—Could I stand by
And see You—freeze—
Without my Right of Frost—
Death's privilege?

Nor could I rise—with You—
Because Your Face
Would put out Jesus'—
That New Grace

Glow plain—and foreign
On my homesick Eye—
Except that You than He
Shone closer by—

They'd judge Us—How—
For You—served Heaven—You know,
Or sought to—
I could not—

Because You saturated Sight—
And I had no more Eyes
For sordid excellence
As Paradise

And were You lost, I would be—
Though My Name
Rang loudest
On the Heavenly fame—

And were You—saved—
And I—condemned to be
Where You were not—
That self—were Hell to Me—

So We must meet apart—
You there—I—here—
With just the Door ajar
That Oceans are—and Prayer—
And that White Sustenance—
Despair—

690

Victory comes late —
And is held low to freezing lips —
Too rapt with frost
To take it —
How sweet it would have tasted —
Just a Drop —
Was God so economical?
His Table's spread too high for Us —
Unless We dine on tiptoe —
Crumbs — fit such little mouths —
Cherries — suit Robins —
The Eagle's Golden Breakfast strangles —
    Them —
God keep His Oath to Sparrows —
Who of little Love — know how to starve —

709

Publication — is the Auction
Of the Mind of Man —
Poverty — be justifying
For so foul a thing

Possibly — but We — would rather
From Our Garret go
White — Unto the White Creator —
Than invest — Our Snow —

Thought belong to Him who gave it—
Then—to Him Who bear
Its Corporeal illustration—Sell
The Royal Air—

In the Parcel—Be the Merchant
Of the Heavenly Grace—
But reduce no Human Spirit
To Disgrace of Price—

712

Because I could not stop for Death—
He kindly stopped for me—
The Carriage held but just Ourselves—
And Immortality.

We slowly drove—He knew no haste
And I had put away
My labor and my leisure too,
For His Civility—

We passed the School, where Children strove
At Recess—in the Ring—
We passed the Fields of Gazing Grain—
We passed the Setting Sun—

Or rather—He passed Us—
The Dews drew quivering and chill—

For only Gossamer, my Gown —
My Tippet — only Tulle —

We paused before a House that seemed
A Swelling of the Ground —
The Roof was scarcely visible —
The Cornice — in the Ground —

Since then — 'tis Centuries — and yet
Feels shorter than the Day
I first surmised the Horses Heads
Were toward Eternity —

721

Behind Me — dips Eternity —
Before Me — Immortality —
Myself — the Term between —
Death but the Drift of Eastern Gray,
Dissolving into Dawn away,
Before the West begin —

'Tis Kingdoms — afterward — they say —
In perfect — pauseless Monarchy —
Whose Prince — is Son of None —
Himself — His Dateless Dynasty —
Himself — Himself diversity —
In Duplicate divine —

'Tis Miracle before me — then —
'Tis Miracle behind — between —
A Crescent in the Sea —
With Midnight to the North of Her —
And Midnight to the South of Her —
And Maelstrom — in the Sky —

754

My Life had stood — a Loaded Gun —
In Corners — till a Day
The Owner passed — identified —
And carried Me away —

And now We roam in Soverign Woods —
And now We hunt the Doe —
And every time I speak for Him —
The Mountains straight reply —

And do I smile, such cordial light
Upon the Valley glow —
It is as a Vesuvian face
Had let it's pleasure through —

And when at Night — Our good Day done —
I guard My Master's Head —
'Tis better than the Eider-Duck's
Deep Pillow — to have shared —

To foe of His—I'm deadly foe—
None stir the second time—
On whom I lay a Yellow Eye—
Or an emphatic Thumb—

Though I than He—may longer live
He longer must—than *I*—
For I have but the power to kill,
Without—the power to die—

762

The Whole of it came not at once—
'Twas Murder by degrees—
A Thrust—and then for Life a chance—
The Bliss to cauterize—

The Cat reprieves the Mouse
She eases from her teeth
Just long enough for Hope to teaze—
Then mashes it to death—

'Tis Life's award—to die—
Contenteder if once—
Than dying half—then rallying
For consciouser Eclipse—

825

An Hour is a Sea
Between a few, and me —
With them would Harbor be —

856

There is a finished feeling
Experienced at Graves —
A leisure of the Future —
A Wilderness of Size.

By Death's bold Exhibition
Preciser what we are
And the Eternal function
Enabled to infer.

861

Split the Lark — and you'll find the Music —
Bulb after Bulb, in Silver rolled —
Scantily dealt to the Summer Morning
Saved for your Ear when Lutes be old.

Loose the Flood — you shall find it patent —
Gush after Gush, reserved for you —
Scarlet Experiment! Sceptic Thomas!
Now, do you doubt that your Bird was true?

875

I stepped from Plank to Plank
A slow and cautious way
The Stars about my Head I felt
About my Feet the Sea.

I knew not but the next
Would be my final inch—
This gave me that precarious Gait
Some call Experience.

883

The Poets light but Lamps—
Themselves—go out—
The Wicks they stimulate—
If vital Light

Inhere as do the Suns—
Each Age a Lens
Disseminating their
Circumference—

887

We outgrow love, like other things
And put it in the Drawer—

Till it an Antique fashion shows—
Like Costumes Grandsires wore.

903

I hide myself within my flower,
That fading from your Vase,
You, unsuspecting, feel for me—
Almost a loneliness.

928

The Heart has narrow Banks
It measures like the Sea
In mighty—unremitting Bass
And Blue Monotony

Till Hurricane bisect
And as itself discerns
It's insufficient Area
The Heart convulsive learns

That Calm is but a Wall
Of unattempted Gauze
An instant's Push demolishes
A Questioning—dissolves.

937

I felt a Cleaving in my Mind—
As if my Brain had split—
I tried to match it—Seam by Seam—
But could not make them fit.

The thought behind, I strove to join
Unto the thought before—
But Sequence ravelled out of Sound
Like Balls—upon a Floor.

986

A narrow Fellow in the Grass
Occasionally rides—
You may have met Him—did you not
His notice sudden is—

The Grass divides as with a Comb—
A spotted shaft is seen—
And then it closes at your feet
And opens further on—

He likes a Boggy Acre
A Floor too cool for Corn—
Yet when a Boy, and Barefoot—
I more than once at Noon
Have passed, I thought, a Whip lash

Unbraiding in the Sun
When stooping to secure it
It wrinkled, and was gone—

Several of Nature's People
I know, and they know me—
I feel for them a transport
Of cordiality—

But never met this Fellow
Attended, or alone
Without a tighter breathing
And Zero at the Bone—

994

Partake as doth the Bee,
Abstemiously.
The Rose is an Estate—
In Sicily.

995

This was in the White of the Year—
That—was in the Green—
Drifts were as difficult then to think
As Daisies now to be seen—

Looking back is best that is left
Or if it be — before —
Retrospection is Prospect's half,
Sometimes, almost more.

1052

I never saw a Moor —
I never saw the Sea —
Yet know I how the Heather looks
And what a Billow be.

I never spoke with God
Nor visited in Heaven
Yet certain am I of the spot
As if the Checks were given —

1066

Fame's Boys and Girls, who never die
And are too seldom born —

1078

The Bustle in a House
The Morning after Death
Is solemnest of industries
Enacted upon Earth —

The Sweeping up the Heart
And putting Love away
We shall not want to use again
Until Eternity.

1093

Because 'twas Riches I could own,
Myself had earned it—Me,
I knew the Dollars by their names—
It feels like Poverty

An Earldom out of sight to hold,
An Income in the Air,
Possession—has a sweeter chink
Unto a Miser's Ear—

1095

To Whom the Mornings stand for Nights,
What must the Midnights—be!

1100

The last Night that She lived
It was a Common Night
Except the Dying—this to Us
Made Nature different

We noticed smallest things—
Things overlooked before
By this great light upon our Minds
Italicized—as 'twere.

As We went out and in
Between Her final Room
And Rooms where Those to be alive
Tomorrow were, a Blame

That Others could exist
While She must finish quite
A Jealousy for Her arose
So nearly infinite—

We waited while She passed—
It was a narrow time—
Too jostled were Our Souls to speak
At length the notice came.

She mentioned, and forgot—
Then lightly as a Reed
Bent to the Water, struggled scarce—
Consented, and was dead—

And We—We placed the Hair—
And drew the Head erect—
And then an awful leisure was
Belief to regulate—

1101

Between the form of Life and Life
The difference is as big
As Liquor at the Lip between
And Liquor in the Jug
The latter — excellent to keep —
But for extatic need
The corkless is superior —
I know for I have tried

1129

Tell all the Truth but tell it slant —
Success in Circuit lies
Too bright for our infirm Delight
The Truth's superb surprise
As Lightning to the Children eased
With explanation kind
The Truth must dazzle gradually
Or every man be blind —

1130

That odd old man is dead a year —
We miss his stated Hat.
'Twas such an evening bright and stiff
His faded lamp went out.

Who miss his antiquated Wick—
Are any hoar for him?
Waits any indurated mate
His wrinkled coming Home?

Oh Life, begun in fluent Blood
And consummated dull!
Achievement contemplating thee—
Feels transitive and cool.

1134

The Wind took up the Northern Things
And piled them in the south—
Then gave the East unto the West
And opening his mouth

The four Divisions of the Earth
Did make as to devour
While everything to corners slunk
Behind the awful power—

The Wind—unto his Chambers went
And nature ventured out—
Her subjects scattered into place
Her systems ranged about

Again the smoke from Dwellings rose
The Day abroad was heard—

How intimate, a Tempest past
The Transport of the Bird —

1138

A Spider sewed at Night
Without a Light
Upon an Arc of White.

If Ruff it was of Dame
Or Shroud of Gnome
Himself himself inform.

Of Immortality
His Strategy
Was Physiognomy.

1158

Best Witchcraft is Geometry
To the magician's mind —
His ordinary acts are feats
To thinking of mankind.

1159

Great Streets of silence led away
To Neighborhoods of Pause —

Here was no Notice — no Dissent
No Universe — no Laws —

By Clocks, 'twas Morning, and for Night
The Bells at Distance called —
But Epoch had no basis here
For Period exhaled.

1206

The Show is not the Show
But they that go —
Menagerie to me
My Neighbor be —
Fair Play —
Both went to see —

1222

The Riddle we can guess
We speedily despise —
Not anything is stale so long
As Yesterday's surprise —

1233

Had I not seen the Sun
I could have borne the shade

But Light a newer Wilderness
My Wilderness has made —

1243

Safe Despair it is that raves —
Agony is frugal.
Puts itself severe away
For its own perusal.

Garrisoned no Soul can be
In the Front of Trouble —
Love is one, not aggregate —
Nor is Dying double —

1337

Upon a Lilac Sea
To toss incessantly
His Plush Alarm
Who fleeing from the Spring
The Spring avenging fling
To Dooms of Balm —

1340

A Rat surrendered here
A brief career of Cheer
And Fraud and Fear.

Of Ignominy's due
Let all addicted to
Beware.

The most obliging Trap
It's tendency to snap
Cannot resist—

Temptation is the Friend
Repugnantly resigned
At last.

1355

The Mind lives on the Heart
Like any Parasite—
If that is full of Meat
The Mind is fat.

But if the Heart omit
Emaciate the Wit—
The Aliment of it
So absolute.

1434

Go not too near a House of Rose—
The depredation of a Breeze
Or inundation of a Dew
Alarm it's walls away—
Nor try to tie the Butterfly,
Nor climb the Bars of Ecstasy,
In insecurity to lie
Is Joy's insuring quality.

1466

One of the ones that Midas touched
Who failed to touch us all
Was that confiding Prodigal
The reeling Oriole—

So drunk he disavows it
With badinage divine—
So dazzling we mistake him
For an alighting Mine—

A Pleader—a Dissembler—
An Epicure—a Thief—
Betimes an Oratorio—
An Ecstasy in chief—

The Jesuit of Orchards
He cheats as he enchants

Of an entire Attar
For his decamping wants—

The splendor of a Burmah
The Meteor of Birds,
Departing like a Pageant
Of Ballads and of Bards—

I never thought that Jason sought
For any Golden Fleece
But then I am a rural man
With thoughts that make for Peace—

But if there were a Jason,
Tradition bear with me
Behold his lost Aggrandizement
Upon the Apple Tree—

1498

Glass was the Street—in tinsel Peril
Tree and Traveller stood—
Filled was the Air with merry venture
Hearty with Boys the Road—

Shot the lithe Sleds like shod vibrations
Emphasized and gone
It is the Past's supreme italic
Makes the Present mean—

1526

His oriental heresies
Exhilirate the Bee,
And filling all the Earth and Air
With gay apostasy

Fatigued at last, a Clover plain
Allures his jaded eye
That lowly Breast where Butterflies
Have felt it meet to die—

1540

As imperceptibly as Grief
The Summer lapsed away—
Too imperceptible at last
To seem like Perfidy—
A Quietness distilled
As Twilight long begun,
Or Nature spending with herself
Sequestered Afternoon—
The Dusk drew earlier in—
The Morning foreign shone—
A courteous, yet harrowing Grace,
As Guest, that would be gone—
And thus, without a Wing
Or service of a Keel
Our Summer made her light escape
Into the Beautiful.

1575

The Bat is dun, with wrinkled Wings —
Like fallow Article —
And not a song pervade his Lips —
Or none perceptible.

His small Umbrella quaintly halved
Describing in the Air
An Arc alike inscrutable
Elate Philosopher.

Deputed from what Firmament —
Of what Astute Abode —
Empowered with what Malignity
Auspiciously withheld —

To his adroit Creator
Ascribe no less the praise —
Beneficent, believe me,
His Eccentricities —

1593

There came a Wind like a Bugle —
It quivered through the Grass
And a Green Chill upon the Heat
So ominous did pass
We barred the Windows and the Doors

As from an Emerald Ghost—
The Doom's electric Moccasin
That very instant passed—
On a strange Mob of panting Trees
And Fences fled away
And Rivers where the Houses ran
Those looked that lived—that Day—
The Bell within the steeple wild
The flying tidings told—
How much can come
And much can go,
And yet abide the World!

1659

Fame is a fickle food
Upon a shifting plate
Whose table once a
Guest but not
The second time is set
Whose crumbs the crows inspect
And with ironic caw
Flap past it to the
Farmers Corn
Men eat of it and die

In Winter in my Room
I came upon a Worm
Pink lank and warm
But as he was a worm
And worms presume
Not quite with him at home
Secured him by a string
To something neighboring
And went along.

A Trifle afterward
A thing occurred
I'd not believe it if I heard
But state with creeping blood
A snake with mottles rare
Surveyed my chamber floor
In feature as the worm before
But ringed with power
The very string with which
I tied him — too
When he was mean and new
That string was there —

I shrank — "How fair you are"!
Propitiation's claw —
"Afraid he hissed
Of me"?
"No cordiality" —

He fathomed me —
Then to a Rhythm *Slim*
Secreted in his Form
As Patterns swim
Projected him.

That time I flew
Both eyes his way
Lest he pursue
Nor ever ceased to run
Till in a distant Town
Towns on from mine
I set me down
This was a dream —

1705

Volcanoes be in Sicily
And South America
I judge from my Geography
Volcanoes nearer here
A Lava step at any time
Am I inclined to climb
A Crater I may contemplate
Vesuvius at Home

1707

Winter under cultivation
Is as arable as Spring

1718

Drowning is not so pitiful
As the attempt to rise.
Three times, 'tis said, a sinking man
Comes up to face the skies,
And then declines forever
To that abhorred abode,
Where hope and he part company—
For he is grasped of God.
The Maker's cordial visage,
However good to see,
Is shunned, we must admit it,
Like an adversity.

1719

God is indeed a jealous God—
He cannot bear to see
That we had rather not with Him
But with each other play.

1732

My life closed twice before its close;
It yet remains to see
If Immortality unveil
A third event to me,

So huge, so hopeless to conceive
As these that twice befel.
Parting is all we know of heaven,
And all we need of hell.

INDEX OF
FIRST LINES

"Faith" is a fine invention [185]
Fame is a fickle food [1659]
Fame's Boys and Girls, who never die [1066]
Glass was the Street—in tinsel Peril [1498]
Go not too near a House of Rose— [1434]
God is indeed a jealous God— [1719]
Good Morning—Midnight— [425]
Great Streets of silence led away [1159]
Had I not seen the Sun [1233]
He fumbles at your Soul [315]
His oriental heresies [1526]
"Hope" is the thing with feathers— [254]
I can wade Grief— [252]
I cannot live with You— [640]
I died for Beauty—but was scarce [449]
I felt a Cleaving in my Mind— [937]
I felt a Funeral, in my Brain, [280]
I had been hungry, all the Years— [579]
I heard a Fly buzz—when I died— [465]
I hide myself within my flower, [903]
I like a look of Agony, [241]
I measure every Grief I meet [561]
I never saw a Moor— [1052]
I started Early—Took my Dog— [520]
I stepped from Plank to Plank [875]
I taste a liquor never brewed— [214]
I think I was enchanted [593]
I tried to think a lonelier Thing [532]
I Years had been from Home [609]
I'm ceded—I've stopped being Their's— [508]
I'm Nobody! Who are you? [288]
I'm "wife"—I've finished that— [199]